I LOVE YOU, SON
WORDS TO HIS SOUL

Copyright © 2017

All rights reserved. Printed in the United States of America. No part of this book may be reproduced or transmitted in any form or by any means, electronic or mechanical, including photocopying, recording, or by any storage and retrieval system, without permission in writing from Hoston Enterprises, LLC and ZL Publishing House, except in the case of brief quotations embodied in critical articles and reviews.

Published by Hoston Enterprises, LLC and ZL Publishing House

Book Cover Design by Emmanuel Gonzales

Interior Design by Christine Borgford, Type A Formatting

A CIP catalog record for this book is available from the Library of Congress.

Hoston, William T.

I Love You, Son / by William T. Hoston.

To contact the author, please visit: ThankGodForToday.com

ISBN-10: 0–692–85565–3
ISBN-13: 978–0-692–85565–2

I Love You, Son

Words to His Soul

William T. Hoston, Sr.

Hoston
Enterprises, LLC

PUBLISHING
HOUSE

DEDICATIONS

To My Mothers, Part I
Mildred H. Hoston, Bertha-Mae Mitchell,
Thelma C. Owens, and Janet Smith

Spades, Poker, and the House of Cards
How many books do you have?/ God dealt me a hand full of face cards with only 4 Spades/ The standard 52/ I still had to bid my hand/ Anything is possible with 4 beautiful Black queens/ Mildred, Bertha-Mae, Thelma, and Janet/ They read me the good book/ Showed me how to make books/ So life wouldn't throw the book at me/ 10-for-2/ Running a Boston/ 200 miles and running is the pace/ When the deck is stacked against you/ Now, how many possibles do you have?/

To My Godmother
Thelma C. Owens
I love you.
A former school principal and teacher, she has spent her entire life educating young people, mentoring them, and raising many as her own. I am also a product of her hard work. One of my Godmother's favorite gospel songs is, I Won't Complain. Some of the lyrics state, "All of my good days/ Outweigh my bad days/ I won't complain." This has been the axiom of her life. Watching my Godmother, I have learned to H.O.P.E.: H.ave O.nly P.ositive E.xpectations for my life.

To My Godfather
Andrew "Sonny" Owens
The only father I have ever known.

I've been knocking on God's door since birth/ My biological father didn't want me/ I prayed to the Holy father/ And "He" gave me a God-father/ To witness my testimony/ A blessing to my world/ Thank you, Daddy/

My biological father was delivered to Hell/ Afterwards, the Devil knocked on my door once, four times, and then three times/ That was his way of saying, "I Love You."/ But I didn't answer/ I just looked out of the peephole as he walked away/

To My Brothers
Feddrick M. Hoston
Release Date: 01/20/2031

Cleveland R. Wilborn
Release Date: 12/21/2019

To My Uncles
Willie A. Holmes
Release Date: 05/14/2020

Recardo J. Holmes
Release Date: Life in Prison

Timothy C. Holmes
Released: 09/16/2013

Acts 3:19: Repent ye therefore, and be converted, that your sins may be blotted out, when the times of refreshing shall come from the presence of the Lord. ~KJV

To My Son
William Terrell Hoston Jr.
You were birthed to fulfill God's purpose for you
and take unconditional care of your mother.
You have the greatest mother in the world.
Daddy loves you.

Your mind will be your greatest tool/ I will teach you/ To keep it free
from enslavement/ What did William T. Hoston Jr. know, and when
did he know it?/ Will be how society defines your legacy/ I love you/
~Ode to W.T.H. Jr.

ACKNOWLEDGEMENTS

All praise to my Lord and savior, Jesus Christ. With Him, all things are possible. He has provided me with the four most influential women in my life, the late Mildred H. Hoston, the late Bertha-Mae Mitchell, Thelma C. Owens, and Janet Smith. I am a product of their hard work and sacrifice. In the words of Abraham Lincoln, "All that I am, or hope to be, I owe to my angel mother[s]."

To my beautiful and darling mother, Janet Smith, your examples of faith, courage, and sacrifice gave me much inspiration over the years to follow my dreams.

To my lovely wife and best friend, Cecilia Hoston, I love you. You have given my life such love, happiness, and joy.

To my nephew, J-Gutta, my rock, I love you.

To the following families: Hoston, Zanders, Owens, Cosby, Mitchell, Duffey, Hooper, Nelson, Veus, Cooper, Franklin, Stewart, Gaines, Robinson, Gauthier, Anderson, Powell, Williams, Campbell, Thomas, Bolling, Hicks, Burrell, Green, Greenup, Hall, Isodore, Trufant, Laurant, Washington, Clements, Vance, Bonner, Sephus, Volley, Calice, Spivey, Wright, Long, Sanders, McQuarters, Baptiste, Davis, Barbre, Lee, Taylor, Carter, Garnett, Watson, Bennett, Swiner, Gabriel, Johnson, Rainey, Lain, Mauricio, and the whole, "132 Villary Street!" #504ForLife. #DTR.

To you whom I have not named, please know that even though you are not named in this book, I deeply appreciate what you have contributed to my life. Your contributions have helped this "Black boy fly."

Children [help to] make your life important. ~Erma Bombeck

CONTENTS

HOPEFUL FUTURE: RAISING A BLACK SON

Objective: The aim of this book is to present my life as a model for my son. Contemporary social science research concerning the positive influence of Black fathers on their Black sons has been understudied. This is in large part because statistics show that the Black man is *missing* leading the majority of Black woman to birth children into a single-parent frame. This six-by-eight can be the start and end. As a result of these statistics with no accurate narrative, the consequential body of literature is presented to be the Black community's moral standing with no regard to build theory on a deeply complex structural and cultural issue.

Background: Fatherhood is the state of being a father, which translates into providing a healthy quality of life for your child. When controlling for race, the term "Black fatherhood" is often followed by "absent" and "deadbeats." Not all Black fathers are absent. Not all Black fathers are deadbeats. Real Black fathers exist.

According to a 2015 *New York Times* article titled, *1.5 Million Missing Black Men,* it was estimated that 625,000 Black men between the ages of 25-to-54 were missing from everyday life because they were either imprisoned or dead. The article posits that missing Black men disrupt the family formation and the molding process of individual children.

Methodology: This research task is approached qualitatively. My son will be a participant observer of my life to make sure that he understands the challenges of Black male life and strives to live a better life than my own. We will be in direct contact with each other. Through the maturation of love my son will investigate both the taken-for-granted assumptions about, and of, my life. He will see my joy and pain. The collection of this data will allow him to identify one major theme: I love him.

Conclusion: My son will fulfill God's purpose for his life and take unconditional care of his mother.

Keywords: Black, Blackness, Black Man, Black Leader, Black Revolutionary, Second Black President
~Hoston, 2016

I LOVE YOU, SON

I tell my son, "I love you" all day, every day/ For him to know that Daddy's love for him is infinite/ Ever since he emerged from the womb/ And placed a never-ending smile on my face/ My life has not been the same/ The ghosts who haunted my past/ Have befriended me/ Casper is no longer my enemy/

I hug and kiss my son all day, every day/ For him to know what Daddy's physical love feels like/ Endless forms of Black male affection/ To create a loving Black male/ And eradicate Black masculine stereotypes/ He won't be too tough to hug Daddy/ He won't be too tough to kiss Daddy/ Our love for each other will be expressive/ I want him to be a bundle of joy/

There will be times/ That I cry when I see my son/ He will ask, "Daddy, why are you crying?"/ My reply will be, "Because I love you, son."/
⁓Hoston, 2017

DEAR GODSON

Dear Godson,
My hope is that one day
You will see me the same way that I see your father

Today, I am doing well for myself
I am a father, educator, coach, and proud college graduate
Due in part to your father

Where I am today is not where I started
Who I am today is not who I used to be

Dear Godson,
Every day will not be sunny
Skies will turn grey

When you are faced with great odds
Know that anything is possible
When you are feeling on top of the world
Know that humility will help you see the world rose-colored

Dear Godson,
As I write this poem, you are still a child
But one day you will be a man with a family of your own

Just as your father is a rock for me
I, too, will be a rock for you
Our circular bond is solid as a rock
~Duffey, 2017

2/18/17

Today, I witnessed your first kiss
Her name was Ella
Ella was 21-months-years-old
A golden child

Her mother and father were not happy :-)

I know you hugged and kissed Ella
Because Mommy and Daddy hug and kiss you
The power of mirroring

I know you hugged and kissed Ella
Because you know love and affection
Two different expressions that bond
The power of affirmation

Today, I witnessed your first kiss
~Hoston, 2017

EARLY IN THE MORNING

It's 4:56 a.m.
You are the best part of waking up.

My son: *Daddy, I want to fly an airplane.*
Thinking to myself: *Take your lil butt back to bed.*

Internalizing his request: I wish we both could *fly far away from here. Where my mind can see fresh and clear.* My mind gravitates from Lionel to Linus as I pull up the security blanket to protect us. I apologize for the world that you were born into which facilitates discrimination, racism, misogyny, sexism, and xenophobia. You were miraculously conceived in 44 days. On the 45th day, God cried. The Immaculate Conception is no more. It's 4 minutes to 5 a.m. and the airplane you want to fly has landed on my shoulders.

My son: *Daddy, I want to fly an airplane.*
Thinking to myself: *I'll help you land safely.*
~Hoston, 2017

THE WINDOW OF OPPORTUNITY

I have been staring through this window all my life/ Gazing beyond the pane/ Leaning against the seal/ Looking for tranquility/

From time to time/ I place my head out of the window/ To clear my mind/ Hoping it blows a wind of courage/

Sometimes the wind blows in an unfamiliar direction/ But in that direction/ I choose to go down a path of the unknown/ Praying it will take me to a place/ I have never been before/ For a newer and richer experience/
~Hoston, 1998

I'VE WAITED MY WHOLE LIFE FOR YOU, PART I

Oh Ceci,

You walked into my life
and erased the invisible lines of doubt

I had built a fortress to protect my heart from the past
and you chiseled away the coated layers of hurt

When you came into my life, certain things had to change
and when you stayed in my life, I changed

Today, I am happy
and tomorrow I will be happier

The disappointment of yesteryear
now gone and forgotten
eternal love for you resides in my heart
every time I think of you
I walk up memory lane
animated about what is forthcoming

Love is the mainstay of our existence
one love, two lives, forever mine
I love you . . .
~**Hoston, 2014**

I'VE WAITED MY WHOLE LIFE FOR YOU, PART II

Oh Ceci,

Time is of the essence
and I know time won't give me time

I'm just a boy named George
and you are just a girl named Cecilia
we met in a culture club

If I had my entire life to live all over again
I pray God would have brought you to me sooner
and I could have loved you much longer

You and me know we got nothing but time
it's the clock of the heart

Today, I am happy
and tomorrow I will be happier

The disappointment of yesteryear
now gone and forgotten
eternal love for you resides in my heart
every time I think of you
I walk up memory lane
animated about what is forthcoming

Love is the mainstay of our existence
one love, two lives, forever mine
I love you . . .
~Hoston, 2014

I GAVE HER A CIRCLE

Sometimes in order to get square with life you have to come full circle/ In a roundabout way I have finally chosen the center of life/ Not the top nor bottom/ The left nor right sides/ Those are the residences of past dwellings/ I have ventured to a new perimeter/ A 360 degree spiritual awakening/ The circumference of my circle is now computed by love/ All points are the same distance from the center/

The radius of my love for her is what is most important/ When we first met/ I tried to fit a square peg into a round hole/ I set selfish boundaries/ And they revolved around a false sense of understanding/ With compassion and a compass/ Thankfully she made her way back to me/ Her love has given my life heroic joy/ My partner in life/ My one true love/ The plane of her love has me going in circles/ When we looked at circles/ I found that no size could measure our love for each other/ In the presence of God/ I will love her, hold her, and honor her/ For all the days of my life/ With this ring I thee wed/ I gave her a circle/
~**Hoston, 2014**

MY VOW OF LOVE

A lot of people say that they have fallen in love at first sight/ But we did/ Your relentless flirting, numerous emails to my work account/ Cyber stalking/ And asking me out on a date/ Drew me in/ Plus there was another guy dressed like Darth Vader from Star Wars flirting with you the day we met/ And I had to save you from him/

We met in a cold Starbucks/ And you warmed my heart/ Our relationship started at 3 years and 6 months/ At least that is what we told people who witnessed our interactions/ After only knowing you less than 48 hours/ I could see the distance between our life span/ Would be closed by our potential love for each other/

The time we were together was spent loving/ And the time we were apart was spent missing/ You spoke to my heart in a way/ No one had before/ Then I responded in a way/ I had never before/

It was my intention to touch you without touching you/ And then by God's grace/ We planted a seed in the earth/ This rain on our wedding day is good luck/ Which symbolizes that our marriage will last forever/ I have waited my entire life for you/ And now I realize that a lifetime with you will not be enough/

I promise to love you/ And take care of you and Junior for the rest of my days/ Thank you for loving me/ And giving me unconditional love/
~Hoston, 2014

TO MY MOTHERS, PART II

It took a Queen of Spades to raise a young Jack/ Surrounded by a Full House/ One-eyed Royals/ My biological mother took the Crown out of the royal purple bag/ Then placed me on the throne/ She Kinged me/ Before I became the King God didn't save/

My life has been a card trick every since/ Shuffle the deck/ Draw a card, any card/ Is this your card?/ No unbeatable hand/ High card/ I made something out of nothing/ Ace in the hole/
~Hoston, 2010

E&J

When the bottle finished spinning
She kissed me and took it with her

That was the last time
We saw each other
15 years ago

She poured her heart out
And left us both empty
~Hoston, 2017

GREATER OF THE TWO . . .

I wish you would choose love over addiction/ For more than a decade you have been out of my life/ Lost/ Not wanting to be found/ Alive/ But playing dead to those who love you/ I pray God resurrects your spirit/ I need more than your Holy Ghost/ All I am/ All I will ever be/ I owe to you/

After more time has passed . . .

I know the conversation will be too difficult to have/ We both wouldn't admit/ We both wouldn't forget/ It would be a clash between love and fear/ The unexpected meets the unknown/ We'll just love with broken hearts/ And allow the embrace to mend the past/

In time/ I hope you choose/ The greater of the two . . .
~**Hoston, 2013**

LISTEN

L-I-S-T-E-N

Be S-I-L-E-N-T

Scrabble the letters. Place them back together. The same result. I need to be heard. By you. Right now.

Children become adults. I'm sorry that you only see me one way and the world sees me in other ways. From this thinking, you will never see my evolution.

How much do I love thee? I love thee to the depths but we birthed each other. You had me and then I had to raise you—*King of the castle.* When you couldn't make it work with HIM, Him, or him, you then took it out on me—*Man of the house.*

Oh let me count the ways we can lose the battles and also lose the war.
~Hoston, 2004

THE NEXT TIME I SEE YOU

The next time I see you/ Your image will be different/ A far cry from how you used to look/ But the tears in my eyes won't let me see that/ The embrace will be familiar/ Like the day I was born/

The next time I see you/ No apologies need to be uttered/ Both of our hearts are sorry/ I've prayed a thousand moments/ I've shed a thousand tears/ I've looked at your picture a thousand times/ And it said back, "I love you," in a thousand ways/

The next time I see you/ I want it to be on this earth/ Seeing you in a casket would break my heart/
~Hoston, 2010

WITHOUT A FATHER

While growing up, the only time my father ever visited me was in the mirror. My reflection was a spitting image. The act of reflecting leads to reflection. After some reflection, he let me down.

He was merely a figment of my imagination. I use to imagine what our lives, my mother and I, would be like if he were a part of it. Those thoughts diminished with age.

Growing up without a father seemed like the norm; therefore, I believed my life was normal. I later realized it wasn't normal. There is nothing normal about a man who lives in quiet desperation and willing to go to the grave without showing love for his children. The Greek philosopher, Plato, on one occasion said that, "We can easily forgive a child who is afraid of the dark; the real tragedy of life is when men are afraid of the light."
~Hoston, 2010

"NO ONE."

Ugly is the soul that leaves
    A front door is only beautiful to strangers knocking
    Those on the other side hear the pain
You are the reason the window blinds are broken
    To look, but not to touch
    Pain from a distance eases the pain up close

Knock, knock
Who's there?
"No one."

Tell Goodbye, I said Hello
    See you later, never
    See you soon, not at all
It is difficult to see a figment of my imagination
    But my imagination has helped me cope with the pain
    Easing your absence
    A lifetime without a father

Knock, knock
Who's there?
"No one."
~Hoston, 2014

ROCKS

My mother threw rocks
My father threw rocks
Both hid their hands

When they turned to look
They had missed me
And hit my son

He is an innocent bystander
Who has never met his attackers
~Hoston, 2017

MY BROTHERS

My greatest failure in life has been the inability to shape, mold, and influence the lives of my two younger brothers, Feddrick and Cleveland.

I have been beating my head against a stonewall
Trying to make sense out of nonsense
But in nonsense there are answers

Could I have done more? And what I did, was that enough?

I began to teach them the game of life
The game has rules they both refused to follow

Feddrick saw how I used to make my paper/ But he chose to manufacture his own/ 25 years in prison for $1,480/ That's a bad return on an even worse investment/ A man is dead/ And two families are destroyed/

Cleveland saw how I used to carry the rock/ But he chose to slang it/ When I was running through the line/ He stayed in the pocket/ Subsequently, the bad decisions of life sacked him/

Could I have done more? And what I did, was that enough?

We all came from 'Him' and different 'Hers'
Children of a fatherless generation

Could I have done more? And what I did, was that enough?

I have dedicated my entire life
To helping young brothers
But I couldn't help my own
~**Hoston, 2010**

MY LATE GRANDMOTHER

My late grandmother, Mildred H. Hoston, was a former educator and dedicated woman of Christ. She told me more positive things than anyone in my life. My grandmother was always upbeat and reassuring. Her favorite saying to me was, "Boy, when you grow up, you gonna be somebody." She encouraged me to read the Bible and find inspirational materials that feed my soul. One of her favorite inspirational readings was, *Our Deepest Fears*, by author, Marianne Williamson (1992). Her favorite excerpt from the passage was the following:

> You are a child of God.
> Your playing small does not serve the world.
> There is nothing enlightened about shrinking
> so that other people won't feel insecure around you.
> We are all meant to shine, as children do.

On November 4, 1997, my grandmother passed away at Phoebe Putney Memorial Hospital in Albany, Georgia. She died in my first semester of graduate school at Florida State University. It is difficult to put into words the impact that her death had on my life. My greatest support system was now gone. She died of Alzheimer's disease, the illness that leads individuals to lose their memory and bodily functions, eventually causing death.

At my grandmother's funeral I compared her to former slave and American abolitionist, Harriet Tubman. Over an eight-year span, Harriet made eight trips to north Philadelphia from the Deep South leading over 300 slaves to freedom. My grandmother was much like Harriet Tubman. She adopted my father, had several foster children, worked with the mentally disabled and handicapped to ensure that they had basic necessities and their bills were paid, and performed her weekly church duties as the First Lady. The passing of my grandmother was not only a loss for me, but also a loss to many people that relied on her services, support, and love. I miss her dearly.

~Hoston, 2010

A NOVELTY

Dear Son,

Let me present to you a short novel about a novelty: **Your great-grandmother, Mildred H. Hoston.** She was the daughter of the late Milton Hooks and Artist Battle-Hooks and wife of the Reverend Reed Hoston Jr.

I'm reminiscing about a place called home. It was on Route 1 in the red dirt plains of Leslie, Georgia. I can't tell you how to get there, but I can show you how to get there. The heart has its own compass. Leslie, Georgia is a tiny dot on the map known for rolling farmland and rumbling tractors. Incorporated in 1892, the town has a population of just over 400 people. It's the kind of town that folks in big cities stop in only to pump gas. They pump, use the restroom, and then leave. But Leslie, Georgia is so much more than farmland and tractors. It is so much more than a rest stop. This diacritical mark on the map once housed in life, and now in death, your great-grandmother.

I remember along the travel to see your great-grandmother was the long highway stretch. Riding along this stretch, you could begin to feel the love permeating. Your great-grandmother's love filled the universe. The universe is an abundant place. But her love could occupy spaces unknown to the seeing-eye. Her love spoke into you. Her love was the reason we believe in the goodness of people. If one paid attention to every detail of how she loved, such a lesson could change the world. She was a school teacher for 35 years, but she was a life teacher and lover of people all her life. God put His hands on her and never took them off.

Before reaching the entrance to her house, there was a narrow gravel road that led to the final destination. There was no doorbell on the house. The crackling of the rocks from the gravel road would alert her to your presence. Down the hill you went. She would eventually appear on the porch. Once you got out of the car, she was always there waiting with open arms. "That's my sweet boy," your great-grandmother would say, echoing her joy to see me to your great-grandfather. From her, I inherited a sense of self-confidence. She was a builder of people—— Hugs, kisses, and words were her tools.

"Hug grandma," she would say with a joyous smile. Once she saw you, you knew a big hug would be waiting. She would give a hug big enough to smother a grizzly bear. You knew a big kiss would be waiting. She would deliver a big kiss on your cheek that smelled like BBQ ribs, collard greens, mac and cheese, and sweet yams—-my favorite meal. "Let grandma see you," she would say.

She never asked, "How much food do you want on your plate?" It was a plate full of food. And she expected you to eat it all.

For dessert, she would serve a homemade blackberry pie with homemade vanilla ice cream. She would always top it with fresh blackberries. In the summer months, the blackberries grew on the trees along the gravel entrance. When I visited during the summer, I would spend many mornings, afternoons, and evenings picking and eating blackberries until my fingers were stained and my belly full from the ripe fruit.

After I licked both plates, she would ask, "Did you have enough, baby?"

"Yes ma'am," I replied. Then we would sit at the table and just talk.

Son, your great-grandmother could ask you about your bad day, and then put her finger under your chin and lift your head up and give you a speech about how tomorrow could possibly be the best day of your entire life. Her message was always: *God is life. Love cures all.* Equally important, she preached: *Be good to people. Find the good people. Be good people.*

I miss her. On my knees, I tell her about you. Like when your mother gave birth. Like when I first held you. Like when you first flipped over on your stomach. Like when you first said, "Daddy." Like when you took your first steps. Like when you kissed Ella. I tell her how you are inquisitive like your Uncle Feddrick and talk all day like your Aunt Jelena. Then I cry for her because she always said good memories should be followed by a good cry. I'm smiling while writing this. I'm crying while writing this. Because I know that meeting you would have brought even more joy to her life.

~Hoston, 2017

MY INFLUENCE

Before they closed the casket/ I made a promise to my grandmother, Mildred H. Hoston/ That I would take my mind out of the gutter and place my head in the books/ So I wouldn't be another young Black male statistic/ Regression/

I became engaged to education/ And we eloped on a philosophical journey/ Doctor of Philosophy/ Since that day/ I haven't cheated on her one time/ With a basketball, a football, a baseball, an 8-ball/ Or a microphone/ Check 1–2, 1–2/

The last time I broke the rack/ The cue ball flew off of the table/ That is how bad I want to scratch my place in his-story/

When they placed the Ph.D. hood on me/ My Niggas in the hood began to believe in me/ I blew a wind of courage to diminish the flames burning from the cross in my front lawn/ I then realized that my life would be O.KKK/ I placed my Bible on the ground/ And then I stood on top of the word/ To God be the glory!/
~**Hoston, 2010**

THE CANDY IS SWEET

My grandmother put the medicine in the candy
When I was sick
She gave me peppermints all day and all night

On her death bed
I fed her peppermint after peppermint
After peppermint after peppermint
During her battle with Alzheimer's disease

My grandmother no longer knew me
But she thanked me for trying to cure her
~Hoston, 2016

RED DIRT HYMN

My grandfather, the Reverend Reed Hoston Jr.
    Was a preacher in the red dirt plains of Georgia

I walked in his shoes, but I didn't walk in his footsteps
    He showed me how to walk by faith and not by sight

Although my calling was different
    The residue from the red dirt
    Left a stain on my heels

He nicknamed me Joshua (Joshua 1:1)
    Telling me that I'd be a servant of the Lord
    Under His command, lead people to the Promised Land
    My grandfather had a vision of me
    Larger than the one I had of myself

In due time, I was hoping that serving the Lord
    Would pay off after a while
    But it took longer than expected because I was afraid
    Fear does the work of reason*ing*

I began flipping through the pages
    Trying to find a verse of explanation
    Hoping for no more bad days

I read the text in red
    But everything in Black
    Made more sense to me

From his grave
> My grandfather professed to me in prayer
> Realize, real lies, with your own real eyes
> For the blind will never follow the correct path

~Hoston, 2008

MR. CURTIS
(of 224 Burton Circle)

Mr. Curtis provided balance to our lives
He beamed with joy
God shined a light on him
From birth to death

His kindness pulled people down to the earth
His smile united them
His love for them made them love each other
These are the true effects of gravity

Mr. Curtis was my mother's father
My grandfather
Our forgotten hero
~Hoston, 2017

THE SKY

When the sky fell
I placed both hands out to catch it

Then I decided to let it slip through my fingers

This decision ultimately allowed me to be human
~Hoston, 2017

" . . . AND I MADE LEMONADE."
(Abbreviated Version)

Unconsciously I float within this stratosphere/ Unable to gain a mind-set/ That would support the inequality of this life/ But consciously sometimes I have hid under the table/ Afraid to emerge/ In fear that those that walk amongst us/ May squash my dreams/

I can't stop the tears from falling/ A White towel hangs within my pocket/ To absorb and surrender/ I often yell into my thoughts/ Trying to figure out a plan/ To stop the wounds from bleeding/

I do not know my fortune/ The fortune given and taken/ And then occupied by a stranger/ A small piece of paper/ In a snail shaped baked cookie/ Manifests the key to my happiness/ This is the year of the Tiger/ My fate is uneven/

The writing on the wall tells the story/ Illustrating that White paint confuses/ More than it amuses the mind/ Big eyes read between the lines/ Entrusting me to decode/ The blue lines that hold this paper captured/ I need to scribble my way out of this bullshit/

Call me the son of the unknown hero/ I sail on the ship of dreams/ Carrying the torch for those who are unable/ The world is my oyster/ But at times I feel I am just a snail/ Awaiting my immersion in salt/

For I search for a handle on this moment/ Wondering what the future holds/ But she released me from her embrace/ Because I carry his name, William Hoston/ Even the Devil was an Angel once/ From the womb we are no longer attached/ She put me out of the cradle/ I am just her son not her baby anymore/

My arms are too short to box with God/ So I stand toe to toe with Jesus/ Demanding that he answers my questions/ And after he slapped some sense into me/ We both sat beneath the crucifix/ And squeezed lemons together/

~Hoston, 1998

TO MY MOTHERS, PART III

From my 4 beautiful Black queens, I learned not to judge.

Years ago, I searched for Jesus and found a homeless man underneath an overpass. The "Son of Man." His shirt faded, jeans worn, and no shoes on his feet. *How did I know he was Jesus? He told me.* Like Jesus he had walked on water; although shallow, he crossed over safely. Like Jesus he was ordered for crucifixions; but death had eluded him. He began a new life in a new body on a new mission. The homeless man was reincarnated in Jesus's image. He explained to me that to live in a state of becoming is the significance of life. Some people seek change and never transform. Others question why change is necessary in the process and never complete the transformation. The homeless man had acquired much knowledge living in isolation. Eventually, the homeless man *became.*

~Hoston, 2010

WHEN I MET MALCOLM

The speaker was impressionable.

In the 9th grade
Malcolm told me we could make money
selling White boys 2 for 5 to White boys
and White girls

He was that Nigga!
Said another way, he was *that* Nigga!

In the 10th grade
Malcolm moved away to make money
selling White girls 12 a key to White boys
and White girls

He was that Nigga!
Said another way, he was *that* Nigga!

In the 11th grade
Malcolm was arrested
posted bail and was released from jail

He was that Nigga!
Said another way, he was *that* Nigga!

In the 12th grade
Malcolm was arrested again
and plead guilty to criminal possession
of a controlled substance

He was that Nigga!
Said another way, he was *that* Nigga!

Translation: *I could have been Malcolm.*
-Hoston, 2011

BUG IN MY EAR

An old Cat/ Once put a bug in my ear/ When it hatched/ I heard/ And I saw life differently/ He said, "Every correction is a change, but not every change is a correction."/ After he blew me that shotgun/ Contact/ He freed me from the shackles on my feet that allowed me to go there but not go there/ There is a message there/ And he answered the real question, "Who is the Nigger?"/

I hung onto every word/ His message led me to Area 51/ A place where the greater minority never have an opportunity to go/ Hidden Fences/ Black extraterrestrials/ Oppressed by the Milky Way/ Dark matter/

This conversation took on a life of its own/ Living and breathing/ And for Black male life/ That is the key to survival / Before being judged by 12, or carried by 6/ The division of life is *two* much to handle/ When we are forced to learn through trial and error/

His final words/ "Don't do good things that look bad."/ Be true to thy self/
~Hoston, 2017

STANDING IN THE MEDIAN:
TOBY WALLER -OR- KUNTA KINTE

One man. Defined two ways.

Passage A: *There is a Toby Waller living inside of me. He is real.* Given the negative institutional roadblocks in American society, think of Toby Waller as a Black male beaten into submission by structural and cultural forces. Generally, the adverse societal and cultural barriers faced are not met with a responsive agenda due to the lack of positive influences, mentors, and outlets. In turn, institutional and systemic racism and discrimination further highlights his struggle because he has not been resourcefully equipped. This Black male is left to cross a faulty bridge to overcome his circumstances. There is limited conscious motivation and, as a result, goals and dreams are redefined to match the definition of success in his environment. In many cases, he finds it difficult to navigate down a path from adolescence to adulthood without proper guidance. Thus, physical, mental, and spiritual liberation is elusive in his quest to become a productive, contributing member within the framework of American society.

Passage B: *There is a Kunta Kinte living inside of me. He is real.* Consider, as a example, Kunta Kinte is a Black male who projects with a sense of indelible pride, pro-Black, heightened level of Black consciousness, identifies with the positive and negative factions of the Black male subculture, and understands the importance of physical, mental, and spiritual liberation. This Black male fights against cultural hegemony to define his own sense of self. These attributes can be generated from positive influences, mentors, and outlets that recognize cultural competence is needed to foster a generational effect on Black males. These positive influences, mentors, and outlets have equipped him. This person now comprehends that a strategic approach is needed to overcome structural and cultural forces detrimental to Black male life.
~Hoston, 2015

HOW TO TREAT A SMASHED FINGER

On December 14, 2007, I graduated with my Ph.D. I had officially entered "a" Caucasian door. On the way in, while pointing in appreciation to the abolitionist who had granted me access, one of the three fingers pointing back at me got smashed in the unlocked door. It was an incredibly painful experience. I proceeded to the restroom to soak my finger in cold water to reduce the swelling. There was a lot to ponder in this moment.

When I returned to the door rather than closing it shut, I left it ajar to allow caution to the wind. Then I placed an emergency key under the mat in case of permanent closure for more to enter.
~Hoston, 2010

ANNA: A.IN'T N.O N.IGGERS A.LLOWED

I killed them. They dead.
"I'm both glad and sorry," said uncle James.

Anna invited them over.
She knows that I hate Niggers.
But she invited them anyway.

I never opened the door.
They wore hoods.

I just shot out of the window.
Bang! Bang! Bang!

I shouted as I pulled the trigger: "Ain't no Niggers allowed here."
"I'm both glad and sorry," said uncle James.

I may have pulled the trigger, but it was their fault.
They are Niggers.

I killed them. They dead.
~Hoston, 2017

WHERE IS JAMES EVANS SR.?

The year 2014 marked the 40th anniversary of the American sitcom, *Good Times*. In 1974, this sitcom introduced the fictional character of James Evans Sr., played by actor John A. Amos Jr., as the golden standard of Black fatherhood. While featured on the sitcom for only three seasons, the magnitude of his character and the show's overall influence on the Black community are both forever sacred. Long before the Black male fathers featured on sitcoms such as *The Cosby Show* (Dr. Heathcliff 'Cliff' Huxtable), *The Fresh Prince of Bel-Air* (Uncle Philip Banks), and *Family Matters* (Carl Winslow), James Evans Sr. stood as the Black community's flagship male role model. He is characteristically described as a strong, Black family man who took honorable measures to protect his family from the pervasive structural and cultural forces that often destroy Black families.

Good Times features lead characters James Sr. and his television wife, Florida Evans (Esther Rolle), along with their three children, James, Jr. "J.J." (James Walker), Thelma (Bern Nadette Stanis), and Michael (Ralph Carter). Each was a star on the show. They lived in apartment 17C in the Cabrini-Green housing projects in Chicago, Illinois. The show was created to feature the family attempting to overcome the structural and cultural burdens of poverty, lack of employment opportunities, family matters, and gangs, which were all importantly addressed in many episodes.

In the early years, the show was a huge success largely in part to the character of James Sr. However, disagreements over the direction of the show coupled with the writers making J.J. a buffoonery type character who fit the typical stereotypes of Black males, did not sit well with the lead actors, Amos and Rolle. Esther Rolle's ire at the show and writers dated back to when they initially wanted to cast her as a single mother of three. She insisted on having a strong, Black male character to provide the show with that needed presence. On the other hand, John Amo's friction came when writers began to marginalize his character and would not allow him to continue to be a strong parental figure. This rift led to his departure, and after three seasons on the show the *CBS* network decided not to renew Amo's contract.

Before leaving the show, the fictional character of James Sr. had made his mark as a pillar of strength for Black males and the family structure. His visibility provided a nuclear family structure in contrast to single-parent households often seen in the Black community. Earlier episodes of *Good Times* did an excellent job of exhibiting how the family, as a social group, was able to overcome serious economic and cultural issues. James Sr. was the stabilizing force that guided the family through those struggles. For example, James Sr. works numerous jobs to provide for the family. On the show he shields J.J. from the influence of Sweet Daddy Williams, the neighborhood loan shark and numbers runner, and from joining the Satan's Knights street gang. He is a symbol of parental security for Thelma and pushes her to be selective in her choice of men. His guidance shows Michael how to channel his pro-Black and rebellious nature.

James Sr.'s life comes full circle in season three when he is reunited with his own father. He did not have a relationship with his father who walked out on the family when James Sr. was a child. In the 1975 episode, *The Family Tree* (Episode 15), Thelma brings the two men together. She finds while doing a family tree project for school that her allegedly deceased grandfather, Grandpa Henry, is still alive. James Sr. had previously told the family that his father was died. Their reunion is met with a painful exchange between father and son who had not seen each other for over 35 years. James Sr. emotionally tells his father, "There is one thought that never crossed my mind and that was walking out [on my family] because I knew how my family was going to feel. So I stayed, man! I stayed!" He continues to tell his father that walking out on the family thrust James Sr. to become the man of the house and he has upheld that role with his own family to ensure that his children have a strong, positive father in their lives.

To this end, the mythical Evans family headed by James Sr. exhibited the importance of having a strong Black masculine presence in the lives of young Black males. The fictional character of James Sr.

showed the world that the growth and development of a young Black male is enhanced through present, active fathering. James Sr. was a television father figure for a generation of young Black males who grew up without one. Decades later, reruns of the show on television allow the world to see the important paternal role he played in the home while attempting to dismantle the negative stereotype of absentee Black fathers. The question that many Black Americans deal with in the real world is, what has happened to the prototype of James Evans Sr. in the Black community?

~Hoston, 2015

IF I RULED THE WORLD

If I ruled the world/ I would push the lead domino/ Causing the rest to fall/ In this analogous space/ We would talk about race/ Get to the root of race/ Solve the problem of race/ And no longer talk about race/ Until we finish the race and complete the task the Lord Jesus has given us/ Acts 20:24/ All fall down from the cross/ Double-six is the spinner/ I would save the world from the bone yard/

If I ruled the world/ Every Caucasian person in the world/ Would turn Black for one day/ And every Black person in the world/ Would turn Caucasian for one day/ Two broken crayons in a box of 64/ That continue to be pitted against each other/ To halt imaginative expression/ Black and White are both Living Parts in a greater Living Whole/

If I ruled the world/ We would be reborn/ So at the end of this day/ We both can die as colorless/
~Hoston, 2016

TO MY MOTHERS, PART IV

Thank you/ For teaching me how to fight with my pen/ I have no deadly weapons/ I am only armed with three degrees and a piece of chalk/ God willing, I'll be able to draw before they draw/ Lead vs. Lead/ To move in a given direction vs. receiving a slug in the back/ Our lives depend on what we aim for/

I do not want to have to sketch my own chalk outline/ With my blood spattered outside of the lines/ The context of a tragic Black male death/ Life told me to "draw inside of the lines" for nothing/ Bad habits die hard/
~Hoston, 2010

DYLANN THE ROOFER

Please forgive any typos, I didnt have time to check it. ~Dylann Storm Roof

While watching the Bowling Green massacre on television/ The roof on the top of Dylann Storm's home began to leak/

After scouring the Internet for answers/ Looking at "How To . . ." websites and videos filled with alternative facts/ Dylann then placed several buckets down/ To avoid getting water on the floor/

When that failed/ He resolved to plug the leaks with bullets/ One by one/ 70 or more shots/ To stop the incoming Black terrain from destroying his home/
~Hoston, 2017

TILL

There are graveyards full of Emmett Till(s)
One White lie = A million died Black bodies

Carolyn Bryant has hid in her privilege for decades/ Hide and seek/
That's the game we play/ But the past is not the past/ When the here
and now/ Demands the truth/

I stand in my own blood/ I am the late Trayvon B. Martin, Michael
Brown Jr., Jordan Davis, Eric Garner, Tamir Rice, Samuel DuBose,
Alton Sterling, and Philando Castile/ All reduced to hashtags/ Archived
to create a fragile Black male psyche/ #WilliamHostonSr is trending
today/ #AddNameHere will be trending tomorrow/

The future looks bleak/ They might as well kill me today/ Put a bullet
in the top of my skull/ Open my mind to understand why American
society does not value Black male life/ Then and now/

A man was lynched yesterday
Another will be lynched tomorrow
~**Hoston, 2017**

MANNN, TALK THAT TALK

In 2016/ The voices of the silent majority were no longer silent/ They spoke loud and clear/ Giving "Us" eight years/ From January 20, 2009 to January 20, 2017/ To believe that "We" mattered/ White guilt/ And then they used the ballot like a bullet/ A 187 to the post-racial myth/ The revenge of the White voter/ A modern day White-lash/ The reckoning of the post-truth/

Mannn, Talk That Talk
They used an American Firearm Icon/ To shoot through the bullet-proof vest of democracy/ And then used Susan B. Anthony's great-great-great granddaughter to cast the fatal vote/ She told the polls one thing/ And then got on the patriarchal pole for Donny/ Pimpin' ain't no illusion/ Where dem dollas at?/ Hold on, Bill is at the bar getting $1's/ Remember, strippers are humans, too/

Mannn, Talk That Talk
Farewell to the CEO of USA, Incorporated/ "Change We Can Believe In" was all a game of Charades/ I'll give you four years/ To act out this word: "Fear."/ Barry's election and presence woke the monster/ Victor Frankenstein's creation is now the POTUS/
~Hoston, 2016

MISEDUCATED RAPPER
(Abbreviated Version)

Microphone Check
1–2, 1–2

Is God a White Racist?/ Beloved Black folks/ This is the Isis Papers/ Native Son dope/ The White Boy[s] Shuffle/ When they see The New Negro/ I Know Why the Cage Bird[s] Sing/ Outside of the project windows/

The Ways of White Folks/ Has planted a Wild Seed/ For the Ex-Colored Man/ Put his Soul on Ice/ And made him an Invisible Man/ In the search for his own identity/ I ask him/ Are you The Help?/ The Butler?/ Or Twelve Years a Slave?/ The preface of life gives purpose/ From Miseducation to Education/ Up From Slavery/

Tar Baby/ The Darkest Child/ The Blacker the Berry/ A Novel of Negro Life/ Untold/ What a blessing/ To Be Young, Gifted and Black/ In this day and time/ Possessing the Secret of Joy/ The Best of Simple/ Leads many to sing the Song of Solomon/ Yet, Miseducated Negroes/ Remain American Slaves/ The Wretched of the Earth/ Do not understand/ That What Looks Like Crazy on an Ordinary Day/ Has been a way of life for the Black masses/

The lesson they must learn/ This is only Half of a Yellow Sun/ The other half descended/ Changing The Color of Water/ A clear and teary stream/ On The Other Side of Paradise/ Is no paradise/ There are only Dust Tracks on a Road/ Another Country/ Than Our America/ The land of The Color Purple/ A place to guide our experiences/ And mold thought/

Inasmuch, What Becomes of the Brokenhearted/ Black men with no guidance/ We pray that Their Eyes Were Watching God/ The Souls of Black Folk/ Narrative of the Life of . . . **A Miseducated Rapper**/ Please learn A Lesson Before Dying/ Words must be conscious of their mission/
~Hoston, 2014

FEBRUARY 11, 1974—R.EST I.N P.EACE

I've lived from February 11, 1974 to the dash/ I live in the dash/ God asked me to punctuate my future/ Therefore, I drew a line in the universe/ To validate my existence/ Flat line to the present/ That was the only way to rise above the depths of my circumstances/ I had a dark past/ But now I have a bright future/ A shining example of 'Why' you should never give up/

I walk with my head held high/ Because I can't see Heaven looking down/ I continue to smile to show life it hasn't disappointed me/ Life is a gift, so I opened it/ And it presented to me the ability to profess my love by helping others/ According to Pablo Picasso/ "The meaning of life is to find your gift/ The purpose of life is to give it away"/ Millions didn't make it/ But I was one of the ones who did/ I owe it to them/ To give the voiceless, a voice/ Those going nowhere, a road to travel/ Those afraid to reach beyond themselves, a ladder to climb/ And those that need to start over, a new beginning/

I live in the dash/ A place past my fears/ My Ph.D. came from being P.oor, H.ungry, and D.etermined/ I continue to take calculated risks/ To prevent my dreams from dying/ So one day, I can happily R.est I.n P.eace with no regrets/
~**Hoston, 2013**

UMBRELLA

Small puddles lie calm
within the crevices of the earth
reflecting on God's trails and tribulations
My own reflection solicits tears to cry down
showering earth's ground
nature breeding manifestation

Raindrops fall heavily
when shed from Angels in Heaven
I can see the clouds of sorrow
Clouds begin to cast
darkening all rays of sunlight
which dawns on the hopes of tomorrow

I'll water Heaven with my tears
when all of my prayers have been said
and God looks down and calls upon me
I'll be able to finally close the umbrella
which has been my protector
to now live life immortally
~Hoston, 1997

TO MY MOTHERS, PART V

The Tragedy of Hamlet/ Life is a series of flawed extremes/ Act 2, Scene 2/ *For there is nothing either good or bad, but thinking makes it so*/ "I love you."/ "I hate you."/ Reality vs. Fiction/ Neither expression carries any weight when the orator has played a small role in your life/ He or she is just eloquent or Godly awful with words/

No Fear Shakespeare/ Act 5, Scene 3/ Life must go on/ *To death, I disguised myself as a madman*/ This is my Shakespearean moment to live forever/ *Be not afraid of greatness*/ Thrive in the moment/ To honor my 4 beautiful Black queens/ To accomplishment this/ *Thou canst not then be false to any man*/
~**Hoston, 2010**

ABOUT THE AUTHOR

DR. WILLIAM T. HOSTON Sr., Ph.D., is a professor, author, motivational speaker, poet, and documentarian who hails from New Orleans, Louisiana. He is associate professor of political science at the University of Houston—Clear Lake. Dr. Hoston holds research interests in the areas of minority voting behavior, political behavior of Black politicians, race and minority group behavior, Black masculinity, sexualities and gender, race and crime, and theories and dynamics of racism and oppression. He has penned a total of eleven books, most recently, *Race and the Black Male Subculture: The Lives of Toby Waller* (2016), *RNIT* (2015, 2016), and *Black Masculinity in the Obama Era: Outliers of Society* (2014).

For more information on Dr. Hoston, please visit:
ThankGodForToday.com